RESIDENT ALIEN

WELCOME TO EARTH!

S.P.

WELCOME TO EARTH!

WRITER
PETER HOGAN

ARTWORK, COLORS, AND LETTERS
STEVE PARKHOUSE

DARK HORSE BOOKS

PUBLISHER
MIKE RICHARDSON

EDITOR
PHILIP R. SIMON

DESIGNER
ADAM GRANO

DIGITAL PRODUCTION
JASON HVAM

This volume collects issues #0-#3 of the Dark Horse Comics miniseries *Resident Alien*, published in 2012. The contents of issue #0 were originally serialized in *Dark Horse Presents* #4-#6, published in 2011.

Published by
Dark Horse Books
A division of Dark Horse Comics, Inc.
10956 SE Main Street
Milwaukie, OR 97222

DarkHorse.com

To find a comics shop in your area, call the Comic Shop Locator Service toll-free at 1-888-266-4226

First edition: February 2013
ISBN 978-1-61655-017-2

10 9 8 7 6 5 4 3 2

Printed in China

ONCE UPON A TIME, THERE WAS AN ALIEN NAMED HARRY...

INTRODUCTION BY PETER HOGAN

I blame Steve Parkhouse. Having collaborated with him long ago on a couple of stories for *The Dreaming*, I was keen to do so again—and anyone who's ever seen Steve's work (on *The Bojeffries Saga* or *The Milkman Murders*, to name but two) already knows the reason why—because he's stunningly good.

Anyway, when Steve told me he wanted to do something involving aliens, I went away and thought about it for a long time. Since the vast majority of stories about aliens have depicted them as the "Bad Guy" (invaders and/or predators), I thought it might make a nice change to feature an alien as "Our Hero." Someone who's basically a nice guy, who doesn't want to invade, probe, or eat anybody—he mainly just wants to go home again. But since he's stuck here on Earth for a while, our alien might well want something interesting to occupy his mind, and what's more interesting than a mystery? Especially a murder mystery. And that's how Harry ended up becoming an amateur detective, albeit a somewhat unusual one.

We introduced our friendly alien to the world in the pages of *Dark Horse Presents* back in 2011, and he starred in his first miniseries a few months later—all of which has now been collected in the volume you're holding in your hands. If you enjoy it, rest assured that you'll be hearing more from Harry and his supporting cast very soon, because this alien is here to stay.

—PETER HOGAN
SOMEWHERE ON EARTH, 2012

IT'S DOWN THIS WAY...
YOU SURE?
UH-HUH. IT'S THE OLD HASKINS CABIN, DOWN BY THE LAKE.

TODAY I DON'T CARE IF HE'S BARON FREAKIN' **FRANKENSTEIN**...

WE **NEED** HIM.

I STILL CAN'T SEE THE POINT OF THIS.
I MEAN, IF YOU WANT TO RELAX, WHY NOT JUST LOOK AT THE VIEW?
AND IF YOU WANT TO EAT FISH, WHY NOT JUST GO AND BUY SOME?
I'LL ADMIT THIS IS RESTFUL, BUT...
ALL THIS APPARATUS IS JUST A DISTRACT--
YOU IN THE ROWBOAT-- THIS IS THE POLICE.
PLEASE PUT YOUR TACKLE DOWN AND COME ON IN TO SHORE.

I KNOW HOW TO ANSWER THIS. IT'S A PHRASE I'VE HEARD ON A THOUSAND T.V. SHOWS...
IS THERE A **PROBLEM**, OFFICERS?
DON'T SEE ME AS I AM. DON'T SEE ME AS I AM. EVERYTHING IS **NORMAL**.

SIR, JUST COME ON IN TO SHORE, PLEASE.
I DON'T WANT TO STAND HERE **YELLING** ALL DAY.
I DO HAVE A **FISHING PERMIT**, IF THAT'S WHAT THIS IS ABOUT...
JUST GET OUT OF THE BOAT, PLEASE.
THEY'RE ON EDGE, JUMPY...**WHY?**

HOW...
...FASCINATING.
...AWFUL.

YEAH, IT WAS A PRETTY MESSY ONE, TOO...
BUT...I DON'T UNDERSTAND...
AM I A SUSPECT?

NO MORE THAN ANYONE ELSE IS RIGHT NOW...NO, THAT'S NOT WHY WE'RE HERE.
I'D LIKE YOU TO TAKE A LOOK AT THE BODY FOR US, IF YOU WOULDN'T MIND.

OH, NO.
BUT... WHY ASK ME?
SURELY YOUR OWN DOCTORS COULD...

WELL, THAT'S OUR PROBLEM IN A NUTSHELL, DOC. SEE, WE ONLY HAD THE ONE DOCTOR IN TOWN...
AND HE'S THE VICTIM.

STATE CORONER WILL BE HERE TONIGHT, BUT RIGHT NOW I COULD DO WITH A LEAD...OF ANY KIND.
THOUGHT MAYBE YOU COULD GIVE THE BODY A QUICK LOOK-SEE...
er...IT'S NOT REALLY MY AREA OF EXPERTISE...
BUT YOU'RE STILL A DOCTOR, AND BESIDES...
FRESH PAIR OF EYES. YOU MIGHT SPOT SOMETHING WE MISSED.
TELL US WHAT YOU THINK?
I CAN'T GET OUT OF THIS...
IF I SAY NO, IT WILL ONLY MAKE THEM SUSPICIOUS...
I...er... SUPPOSE SO...
'PRECIATE IT, DOC...WE'LL HAVE YOU BACK WITH THE FISHES IN NO TIME AT ALL, PROMISE.
THREE YEARS AGO
I CAN DO THIS...

I HAVE EQUIPMENT...
I CAN SURVIVE.
I CAN PASS AS ONE OF THEM...
BUT I MUST BE CAREFUL.
NOT TO GET INVOLVED. TO KEEP MY DISTANCE.
AND KEEP MY HEAD DOWN...
ALL THOSE YEARS OF HIDING, AND NOW...
SORRY YOU'VE GOTTA RIDE IN THE BACK, DOC.
MIND YOUR HEAD.
POLIC
I'M TRAPPED.

CALM,
CALM,
CALM...
YOU OKAY BACK THERE, DOC?

I'M FINE, BUT...
YOU KNOW, I COULD HAVE JUST FOLLOWED BEHIND YOU IN MY TRUCK...

DON'T WORRY ABOUT IT. WE'LL GET YOU SAFE HOME AGAIN.
SO... VANDERSPEIGLE... THAT A GERMAN NAME?

DUTCH, ACTUALLY.
ORIGINALLY, THAT IS...DO WE HAVE FAR TO GO, TO THE CRIME SCENE?

NOPE, NOT FAR AT ALL. DOC HODGES WAS MURDERED AT HIS CLINIC...
JUST THE OTHER SIDE OF TOWN.

Patience WELCOMES CAREFUL DRIVERS

The Great O

TENTS · STOVE

CAN'T EVEN **REMEMBER** THE LAST TIME WE HAD A MURDER IN THESE PARTS.

HERE IT IS... DOC HODGES'S CLINIC...
CLOSEST THING TO A HOSPITAL FOR NIGH ON A HUNDRED MILES.
POLICE

NO SIGN OF THE CORONER'S VAN.
YEAH, I GOT EYES, DELBERT.
OUT YOU COME, DOC.

ASTA, HONEY...
YOU HOLDING UP OKAY?

NO.
I'M REALLY NOT.
WHAT DID YOU THINK?
DOC HODGES WAS LIKE A FATHER TO ME. HE...
What?

SORRY, ASTA-- THIS IS DR. HARRY VANDERSPEIGLE...
HE'S COME TO HAVE A LOOK AT THE DECEASED FOR US. DOC, THIS IS ASTA, ONE OF OUR NURSES. SHE'S THE ONE FOUND THE BODY.

WHY DON'T YOU TAKE OFF NOW? YOU LOOK ALL IN...
I CAN'T. I HAVE TO--
IT'S FINE. I'LL GET ONE OF THE OTHER GIRLS TO COVER FOR YOU.

WELL... IF YOU'RE SURE...
BODY'S ROUND THE BACK, DOC.
ASTA, YOU DIDN'T TOUCH ANYTHING, DID YOU?

I...DID PUT A SHEET OVER HIM.
IS THAT OKAY?

I DIDN'T WANT THE FLIES TO GET AT HIM...

OKAY, THEN...
THE VICTIM WAS A WHITE MALE, AGED IN HIS EARLY SIXTIES...
THIS IS FASCINATING.

THAT MUCH WE ALREADY KNOW, DOC...AND HE WAS SIXTY-TWO.
YES, OF COURSE...
VERY WELL...LET'S SEE IF I CAN TELL YOU ANYTHING NEW.

THE KILLER WAS PROBABLY RIGHT HANDED AND TALL--TALLER THAN THE VICTIM, ANYWAY--AND HE ATTACKED FROM BEHIND.
HOW CAN YOU TELL?
PARTLY BY THE WOUND.
SEE? THE CUT IS ANGLED UPWARDS AND GOES FROM LEFT TO RIGHT...CAUSED BY A SERRATED BLADE... COULD BE A HUNTING KNIFE OR A CARVING KNIFE...

THERE ARE NO CUTS ON THE VICTIM'S ARMS, SO HE WASN'T TRYING TO DEFEND HIMSELF FROM A FRONTAL ATTACK...
ALSO, THE BLOOD SPATTER GOES FORWARDS FROM THE BODY, AND IT'S UNINTERRUPTED. THERE WAS NO OBSTACLE--LIKE A PERSON--IN ITS WAY.

ONCE HE WAS DEAD, THE KILLER JUST DROPPED HIM, AND THE BODY FELL BACKWARDS LIKE THIS.
SOUNDS LIKE YOU GOT SOME FORENSIC EXPERIENCE, DOC.

NO, NOT REALLY. I'M JUST...
OBSERVANT, I SUPPOSE...

ANY CHANCE YOU COULD GIVE ME A TIME OF DEATH?

JUDGING BY LIVIDITY...AROUND MIDNIGHT IS MY GUESS...
THOUGH AN AUTOPSY SHOULD TELL YOU MORE, OF COURSE.
YES, THIS IS FASCINATING...BUT I MUSTN'T GET SEDUCED BY IT. TIME TO EXTRICATE MYSELF.

WELL, THANKS FOR THAT, DOC. AT LEAST IT GIVES ME SOMETHING TO WORK ON...
HAPPY TO HELP, BUT...
CAN I GO NOW? I MEAN, COULD YOU GIVE ME A RIDE HOME AGAIN, PLEASE?
DR. VANDERSPEIGLE, I PRESUME?
THE POLICE TOLD ME THEY WERE HOPING TO ENLIST YOUR HELP...A PLEASURE TO MEET YOU, SIR.
CUTHBERT C. HAWTHORNE AT YOUR SERVICE...FOLKS CALL ME BERT.
BERT'S THE MAYOR OF PATIENCE, DOC.
WATCH YOUR STEP-- HE'S A SLICK ONE.
IT'S HARRY, ISN'T IT? CAN I CALL YOU HARRY?
er... YES, OF COURSE...
HARRY, DOC HODGES'S PASSING IS A SAD LOSS FOR OUR LITTLE COMMUNITY. A GOOD MAN. HE'LL BE SORELY MISSED.
BUT HE'S LEFT US IN SOMETHING OF A BIND. IT'LL PROBABLY TAKE MONTHS TO REPLACE HIM...

MEANWHILE, ALL I'VE BEEN ABLE TO RUSTLE UP IN THE WAY OF TEMPORARY HELP IS SOME SNOT-NOSED KID WHO'S PRACTICALLY AN INTERN...
AND EVEN HE CAN'T GET HERE TILL NEXT WEEK, SO I WAS HOPING YOU COULD...

OH, NO...
NO, PLEASE... I COULDN'T POSSIBLY...
I MEAN, I'M A SPECIALIST... I'VE NEVER BEEN IN GENERAL PRACTICE...

I MEAN, I'M NOT GOOD WITH PEOPLE...
AND BESIDES, I HAVE ALL MY OWN WORK TO DO AND...
OH, THE NURSES WILL HELP YOU WITH THAT, AND IT'S ONLY FOR A WEEK OR SO...
YOU'LL BE GENEROUSLY PAID, AND...

HARRY, DO I REALLY HAVE TO BRING UP YOUR HIPPOCRATIC OATH?
THE PEOPLE OF THIS TOWN GET SICK AND HAVE ACCIDENTS AND BABIES, AND RIGHT NOW THEY NEED YOU. SO...WHADDAYA SAY?

WHAT CAN I SAY? THIS JUST GETS WORSE AND WORSE...
ALL RIGHT. I'LL DO IT...
BUT ONLY FOR A WEEK.
HE SAID YES, BOYS!
TOLD YOU HE WAS SLICK, DOC.

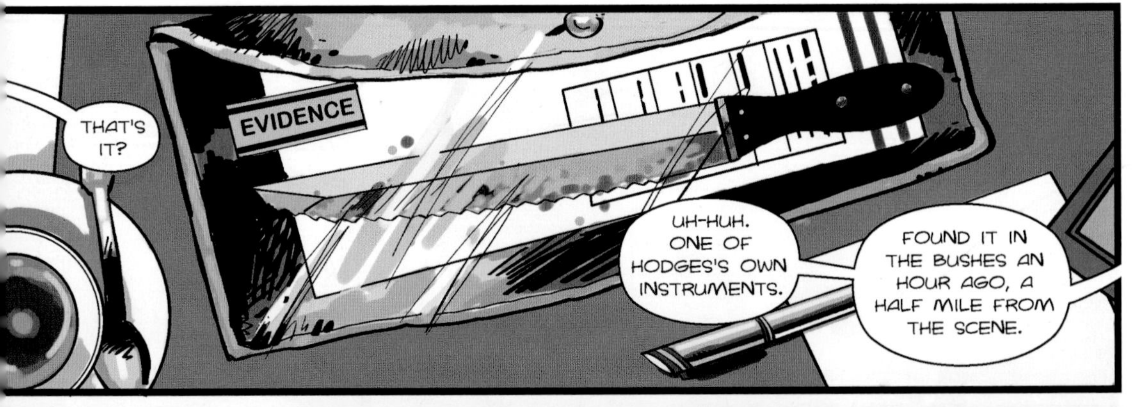
EVIDENCE
THAT'S IT?
UH-HUH. ONE OF HODGES'S OWN INSTRUMENTS.
FOUND IT IN THE BUSHES AN HOUR AGO, A HALF MILE FROM THE SCENE.

"MY GUESS IS THE KILLER GOT INTO THE HOUSE, THEN HODGES FOUND THE BACK DOOR OPEN AND WENT OUT ONTO THE PORCH TO INVESTIGATE...
"AND THE KILLER FOLLOWED HIM OUT THERE."

WAS ANYTHING STOLEN?
YEAH...NURSES ARE STILL DOING AN INVENTORY, BUT IT LOOKS LIKE A WHOLE BUNCH OF PILLS ARE MISSING.
COULD BE THE THIEF **PANICKED** WHEN HE SAW HODGES.

THERE ANY **PRINTS** ON THAT THING?
HOPE SO.
LAB'S PICKING IT UP ANYTIME NOW.

WELL, THAT'S **SOMETHING**.
I JUST HOPE YOU SOLVE THIS ONE BEFORE WE END UP WITH A **THIRD** BODY ON OUR HANDS, MIKE. WE--

NO.
THERE'S ONLY BEEN ONE OTHER KILLING. WALTER MAYHEW WAS AN ACCIDENT.
HE GOT HIMSELF BLIND-DOG WASTED ON HOMEMADE HOOCH AND FELL ON A SCYTHE.
END OF STORY.
"FELL ON A SCYTHE..."
YOU STILL BUY THAT? EVEN AFTER HODGES?
WE FOUND WALTER'S JUG.
AND THE STUFF INSIDE WOULD'VE POLEAXED A GRIZZLY.
ACCIDENT. THAT'S MY OFFICIAL LINE ON THE MATTER, BERT...AND YOU BETTER PLAY ALONG...
BECAUSE IF THE PRESS START THINKING WE'VE GOT A SERIAL KILLER ON OUR HANDS, YOU CAN KISS THE TOURIST SEASON GOODBYE. MAYBE NEXT YEAR'S, TOO.

NO... AND I'M NOT LOOKING FORWARD TO IT, EITHER...

Patience POLICE

IT'S BEEN FOUR DAYS NOW...

...AND BERT SEEMS TO BE AVOIDING MY ***CALLS***...

I SUSPECT THAT MY REPLACEMENT HAS FALLEN THROUGH FOR SOME REASON AND BERT DOESN'T KNOW HOW TO TELL ME...

SO I SHALL HAVE TO PRETEND TO BE ANGRY, AND LET HIM SWEET-TALK ME INTO STAYING ON...

...BECAUSE THE TRUTH IS...

...I DON'T ACTUALLY ***MIND***.

BUT TO ME THEY ARE *TRANSPARENT*.
1/2 PRICE!
EVERY MICROMOVEMENT OF MUSCLE AND NERVE, EVERY CHANGE OF PUPIL SIZE TELLS ME THE *REAL* STORY...
AND THEIR HANDS ARE SO...*ELOQUENT*.

THE WAY THAT MIKE'S ALWAYS STRAY TOWARDS HIS STOMACH...
...TRYING TO HIDE THE SLIGHT HERNIA THAT HE WORRIES ABOUT NEEDLESSLY.
WHILE THE SLIGHT ABRASIONS ON BERT'S WRISTS SPEAK VOLUMES ABOUT HIS FONDNESS FOR MILD BONDAGE...

ALL THEIR LITTLE SECRETS ARE AN OPEN BOOK.
BUT WHAT ABOUT THE *BIG* SECRETS?

dial M for Murder
COULD HODGES'S KILLER HIDE HIS GUILT FROM *ME?*

I'D LIKE TO RENT THIS ONE, PLEASE...
AND I'VE GOT ONE TO RETURN AS WELL.
PANTERA

YOU SURE LIKE YOUR MURDER MYSTERIES, DON'T YOU, DOC?

YES...
I ALWAYS LIKE TO TRY TO WORK OUT WHO THE KILLER IS.

I WONDER... **COULD** I?
COULD I **REALLY?**

THIS IS FOOLISHNESS.
JOE'S DINER
DINNER, THEN BACK TO THE CLINIC.

I SHOULDN'T GET INVOLVED. TOO RISKY.
ALTHOUGH... I PROBABLY HAVE BEEN TOO CAUTIOUS.
IN TRAINING, THEY TOLD ME THAT MY MENTAL POWERS SIMPLY WOULDN'T WORK ON SOME HUMANS, THAT THEY'D SEE ME AS I REALLY AM...
BUT THE ESTIMATE WAS VERY LOW...
JUST ONE IN A MILLION...
THAT'S ONLY SIX THOUSAND PEOPLE ON THE WHOLE PLANET.
SO THE ODDS OF ONE OF THEM TURNING UP HERE MUST BE--
FREEZE RIGHT THERE...

COME ONE STEP CLOSER AND I'LL BLOW YOUR *%@★ING HEAD OFF...
I MEAN IT.

ASTA, IT'S **ME**...DR. VANDERSPEIGLE...

...WE MET THE OTHER DAY.

PLEASE... PUT THE GUN **DOWN**.

OH...
GEEZ, DOC... I'M SO **SORRY**...
I COULDN'T SEE YOU THAT CLEARLY...

IT'S JUST, I'M OUT HERE ALL ALONE, AND... AFTER WHAT HAPPENED TO DOC...
WHEN I HEARD A NOISE, I...**PANICKED**, I GUESS.

I UNDERSTAND. YOU'VE BEEN UNDER A LOT OF STRESS, BUT...
...CAN WE PUT THE GUN **AWAY** NOW, PLEASE?

SURE. IT'S THE DOC'S OLD HUNTING RIFLE.
WASN'T EVEN LOADED.
SO... YOU'RE WORKING TONIGHT?

YEAH. IT'S MY FIRST SHIFT SINCE...
SINCE...

LET'S GO TO THE KITCHEN, SHALL WE?
I'LL MAKE US SOME COFFEE.

ON SECOND THOUGHT, I THINK WHAT *YOU* NEED IS SOME CHAMOMILE TEA...
IT SHOULD HELP TO RELAX YOU.
I'LL GIVE IT A TRY.

YOU SEEM TO KNOW YOUR WAY AROUND HERE PRETTY WELL...
YES, I MOVED INTO THE GUEST ROOM A FEW DAYS AGO.
EASIER THAN DRIVING BACK AND FORTH TO MY PLACE ALL THE TIME.

HERE YOU GO...
THANKS.
LET'S HOPE IT'S *QUIET* TONIGHT.

IT'S BEEN QUIET EVERY NIGHT I'VE BEEN HERE.
I WAS WONDERING WHY WE EVEN NEED A NIGHT NURSE.

WELL, *MOSTLY* THAT'S THE WAY IT IS.
I USUALLY SPEND MY SHIFT DOZING ON THE COUCH AND WATCHING OLD HORROR MOVIES...

...BUT SOME NIGHTS IT GETS ROUGH--JUST NONSTOP EMERGENCIES...
CAR ACCIDENTS, BAR FIGHTS, THAT KIND OF THING.

SOMETIMES A HIGH-SCHOOL KID'LL GET SO OUT OF IT ON SOMETHING THAT THEIR FRIENDS GET WORRIED AND DUMP THEM ON OUR PORCH TO HAVE THEIR STOMACH PUMPED.
GET QUITE A FEW BIRTHS IN THE EARLY HOURS, TOO.

ONE NIGHT ALL THE NURSES GOT CALLED IN TO HELP OUT WITH A DIFFICULT ONE, AND THE DOC ENDED UP DOING A C-SECTION.
WHICH WAS KIND OF GROSS, BUT FASCINATING. THE HUSBAND PASSED OUT.

OKAY, I TAKE IT ALL BACK. I DO NEED YOU HERE.
DO YOU ENJOY THE WORK?

YEAH, I REALLY DO.
IT'S NICE TO MEAN SOMETHING, Y'KNOW? TO MAKE A DIFFERENCE...

YES, I KNOW WHAT YOU...
ASTA, ARE YOU **OKAY?**

YEAH, IT'S JUST... MY **VISION** KEEPS BLURRING.
MAYBE I NEED TO GET MY EYES TESTED...

YOU'RE PROBABLY JUST TIRED.
HOW'VE YOU BEEN SLEEPING LATELY?

YEAH, NOT SO MUCH.
THEN I'M ORDERING YOU TO GO AND CATCH A FEW HOURS ON THE COUCH... **WITHOUT** THE T.V.
I'LL WAKE YOU IF I NEED YOU.

THANKS, DR. VANDER... VANDERSP...

CALL ME DOC, OR HARRY.
EITHER ONE'S EASIER TO PRONOUNCE.

MIKE...
WHAT CAN I GET YOU?
NO THANKS, LARRY--JUST NEED TO TALK TO ONE OF YOUR CLIENTELE.

A **WORD**, IF YOU PLEASE.

CHIEF.
WHAT'S UP?

DOWNLOAD, I DON'T HAVE THE TIME OR THE ENERGY TO BUST YOU FOR SUPPLYING STUFF THAT ISN'T EXACTLY LEGIT TO ALL THE SUCKERS THAT WANT IT...
BUT I COULD ***FIND*** THE TIME.

SO?
SO I NEED INFORMATION.

YOU KNOW ALL THE WILD KIDS IN TOWN, BETTER THAN I DO.
ANY OF 'EM FOOL ENOUGH TO BREAK INTO A DOCTOR'S OFFICE LOOKING FOR PILLS?

I GUESS, MAYBE...
WAIT...YOU SAYING SOME KID KILLED HODGES?

KINDA LOOKS THAT WAY.

LISTEN, IF THAT'S TRUE, THEN THEY'LL BE RUNNING SCARED SOMEWHERE OUT THERE--
AND SOONER OR LATER I WILL GET TO HEAR ABOUT IT.
BE HAPPY TO PASS THAT ON. HODGES WAS A GOOD MAN.

YEAH, HE WAS.
YOU HEAR ANYTHING AT ALL, YOU TELL ME.

I THOUGHT THE KILLER MIGHT **BE** HERE, BUT...I SENSE NOTHING OUT OF THE ORDINARY. NO ANGER, NO REMORSE, NO GUILT...

WE THEREFORE COMMIT HIS BODY TO THE GROUND. EARTH TO EARTH, ASHES TO ASHES, DUST TO DUST...

JUST WAVE AFTER WAVE OF **SORROW**.

AMEN.

WELL, THAT'S **THAT**.
I'M HAVING SOME FOLKS BACK TO MY PLACE FOR SNACKS AND DRINKS.
YOU COMING?
BETTER NOT. TOO MUCH TO DO.

WHAT HAPPENED WITH THE WEAPON? THE **FINGERPRINTS**, I MEAN...
NO LUCK. TOO SMUDGED.

WHAT ABOUT THE BURGLARY ANGLE?
I'M **WORKING** ON IT.

AND RIGHT NOW **YOU'VE** GOT **ANOTHER** PROBLEM TO WORRY ABOUT.
AH...
THIS **COULD** BE A LITTLE AWKWARD.

HARRY...
GOOD OF YOU TO COME.

I FELT I SHOULD PAY MY RESPECTS.
ARE ANY OF HIS FAMILY HERE?

NO, NO FAMILY.
MARGE--THAT WAS HIS WIFE--DIED A FEW YEARS AGO. DIDN'T HAVE ANY KIDS...AND NO OTHER FAMILY THAT I KNOW OF. LISTEN, HARRY...I'M SORRY I HAVEN'T RETURNED YOUR CALLS, BUT--

IT'S FALLEN THROUGH, HASN'T IT?
THE REPLACEMENT YOU HAD LINED UP.

er... YES, AS A MATTER OF--
ANOTHER WEEK.

I'M SORRY?
I'LL COVER THINGS FOR ANOTHER WEEK...
BUT YOU HAVE GOT TO ORGANIZE SOMEONE TO TAKE OVER BY THE END OF THAT. CLEAR?

OH, ABSOLUTELY.
YOU'RE A PRINCE, HARRY. I'LL GET RIGHT ON IT...BUT RIGHT NOW I MUST FLY. I HAVE GUESTS DUE AT MY HOUSE...

BUT WHAT AM I SAYING? YOU MUST COME ALONG, TOO-- IN FACT, I INSIST...
NO-- THANK YOU, BUT NO.
I'M NOT...GOOD AT SOCIAL EVENTS. THEY MAKE ME UNCOMFORTABLE.

THEN I'LL SEE YOU OUT AT THE CLINIC SOME-TIME...
HODGES BEQUEATHED THE WHOLE PLACE TO THE TOWN, BUT...IT LOOKS LIKE IT'S DOWN TO ME TO SORT THROUGH ALL HIS PAPERS AND BELONGINGS.

I'M A LAWYER BY TRADE, BUT I'VE NEVER GOTTEN USED TO DOING STUFF LIKE THAT.
IT FEELS LIKE PRYING, SOMEHOW... AND YOU NEVER KNOW WHAT YOU'LL FIND.

AWRIGHT, AWRIGHT...
I'M COMING.

OW.
HEY!
RUFUS ROBERTS...

AND A BIG PILE OF PILLS.
WHY AM I NOT SURPRISED?

HEY, YOU WANT SOME? WE CAN DEAL.
NO NEED TO GET--

LISTEN, YOU LITTLE $#%&...
I KNOW WHERE YOU GOT THIS STUFF...AND I KNOW YOU KILLED A DECENT MAN TO GET IT.

I DIDN'T, I DIDN'T, I SWEAR...
PLEASE ...STOP...

TALK.
WHAT HAPPENED TO HODGES?
I DON'T KOFF KNOW.

I GOT IN THROUGH A WINDOW...FOUND THE PILLS...THEN I SAW THE KOFF BACK DOOR WAS OPEN...
THE OLD MAN WAS OUT THERE...DEAD... AND COVERED IN KOFF BLOOD.

SO I GRABBED THE STUFF AND SPLIT, FAST AS I KOFF COULD. THAT'S IT, I SWEAR...

OKAY, NOW YOU'RE GONNA TELL ALL THAT TO THE COPS.
NO, I... DUDE!
WHAT ARE YOU DOING?

SORRY, KID ...SOME THINGS ARE JUST TOO BIG TO HIDE.
IT'S DOWNLOAD. GIMME THE CHIEF.

OW.
HOLD STILL, PLEASE.

WELL, YOU DON'T NEED ANY STITCHES.
A SIMPLE BAND-AID SHOULD DO THE TRICK.

HE WAS LIKE THAT WHEN WE BROUGHT HIM IN, DOC.
HONEST.

THAT RIGHT, MR. ROBERTS?
WHO DID HIT YOU?
THESE DRUGGIE TYPES ARE ALWAYS FIGHTING AMONG THEMSELVES.
SEE IT ALL THE TIME.

I AIN'T SAYING A WORD TILL I GET A LAWYER...
EXCEPT I'M INNOCENT, IS ALL.

CAN YOU GIVE ME SOMETHING FOR THE PAIN, DOC?
I'LL GIVE YOU A COUPLE OF PILLS, BUT THAT'S ALL.

YOU'RE AN ADDICT, MR. ROBERTS... AND GIVEN YOUR CIRCUMSTANCES, NOW MIGHT BE A VERY GOOD TIME TO QUIT.
I'LL TALK TO THE CHIEF, SEE IF WE CAN GET YOU ON SOME KIND OF PROGRAM.

YOU WANT TO HELP ME? CONVINCE THEM...
I STOLE THE PILLS, SURE ...BUT I'M NOT A KILLER.

I DIDN'T DO IT, DOC ...YOU GOTTA BELIEVE ME.
OH, I DO, MR. ROBERTS.
BECAUSE I CAN TELL THAT YOU'RE NO MORE THE KILLER THAN I AM.

EVERYTHING OKAY?
HE'S FINE.
JUST A MINOR CUT AND SOME BRUISING.

WELL, THANKS FOR COMING DOWN.
LAST THING I NEED IS HIM ACCUSING **US** OF DOING IT.

HE **SAYS** HE'S INNOCENT.
SURE.
THEY **ALL** SAY THAT.

EVERY CROOK, GRIFTER, AND LOWLIFE TRASH I'VE EVER ARRESTED HAS BEEN AS INNOCENT AS A NEWBORN LAMB.
KINDA WONDER IF I'LL **EVER** MEET A GUILTY ONE.

OH, HE ADMITS TO STEALING THE PILLS--BUT NOT TO KILLING HODGES.
YOU REALLY THINK HE **DID** IT?

THE PILLS WERE STOLEN FROM THE CLINIC THE SAME NIGHT THAT HODGES DIED. PLUS THE KID LEFT PRINTS ALL OVER THE PLACE.
THAT'S **MORE** THAN ENOUGH TO CHARGE HIM, SOON AS I TALK TO THE D.A. HE'S ALSO TALLER THAN HODGES, JUST LIKE YOU SAID.

IN FACT, THE FORENSICS GUYS PRETTY MUCH BACKED UP EVERYTHING YOU TOLD US.
HOPE I CAN CALL ON YOU AGAIN, IF EVER I NEED TO.

OF COURSE, BUT...
I CAN'T HELP WONDERING IF ROBERTS **COULD** BE TELLING THE TRUTH.

THEN WHO KILLED HODGES?
IT'S NOT LIKE THERE ARE ANY **OTHER** SUSPECTS AROUND.

NAH, ROBERTS **FITS**.
EXIT
HODGES CAUGHT HIM STEALING, AND HE PANICKED. END OF STORY.

HOME.

EVERY NIGHT I LOOK UP AND I WONDER THE SAME THINGS...

DID YOU HEAR ME?

ARE YOU COMING?

HEY, DOC...

YOU WISHING ON A STAR?

SOMETHING LIKE THAT.

IS THAT COFFEE I SMELL?

JUST MADE A POT.

I'LL POUR YOU ONE.

THANKS. I NEED IT.

ELLEN, YOU'VE WORKED HERE A LONG TIME...
FOREVER, FEELS LIKE.

WHAT WAS HODGES LIKE?

A GOOD MAN. GOOD DOCTOR, TOO.
COURSE, HE GOT A LOT CRANKIER AFTER HIS WIFE DIED, BUT WE ALL CUT HIM SOME SLACK FOR THAT.

HE LIVED HERE ALL HIS LIFE, DIDN'T HE?
YUP. BORN, BRED, AND BUTTERED, AS MY DAD USED TO SAY.
MY MOM WENT TO SCHOOL WITH HIM.

DID HE HAVE ANY ENEMIES, THAT YOU KNOW OF?

NO, OF COURSE NOT.
SERIOUSLY, WHO HAS ENEMIES?

ANYWAY, I THOUGHT THAT GUY YOU WERE JUST TREATING WAS THE DOC'S KILLER...
WHO TOLD YOU THAT?
HIS HONOR THE MAYOR, ABOUT TWENTY MINUTES AGO. HE'S STILL UPSTAIRS, SAID HE'D COME TO CLEAR OUT DOC'S STUFF.

NOW?
OH WELL, I SUPPOSE I'D BETTER GO SAY HELLO. YOU OKAY DOWN HERE?
SURE. IT'S ANOTHER QUIET NIGHT.

YOU ASK ME, THE CRAZIES ARE JUST SAVING IT UP FOR THE FULL MOON.
BERT? YOU UP THERE?
IN HERE.

I DIDN'T EXPECT TO FIND ***YOU*** HERE THIS LATE...
COULDN'T SLEEP, DEAR BOY, COULDN'T SLEEP.

I SUPPOSE I'M ***ELATED***, NOW THAT MIKE'S CAUGHT THE KILLER.
I TELL YOU, IT'S A REAL ***LOAD*** OFF.

I MEAN, FOR A **WHILE** THERE I THOUGHT WE WERE DEALING WITH A SERIAL KILLER, AND--
REALLY?
WHY WOULD YOU THINK THAT?

OH, A FARMER DIED LAST MONTH. MIKE ASSURED ME IT WAS AN ACCIDENT, BUT WHEN HODGES WENT **TOO**...
WELL, I GUESS I LET MY IMAGINATION RUN A LITTLE WILD.

BUT FORTUNATELY, MIKE WAS **RIGHT**, AND NOW IT'S ALL SEWN UP NICELY.
YOU OKAY, HARRY? YOU SEEM TIRED...

IT'S JUST... BEEN A LONG DAY, THAT'S ALL.
SO WHAT ARE YOU DOING WITH ALL THIS STUFF?

OH, JUST TRYING TO SORT THINGS INTO TWO PILES. ONE FOR THE TRASH, ONE FOR THE GOODWILL.
HELLUVA WAY TO SUM UP A **LIFE**, ISN'T IT?

HIS HIGH-SCHOOL YEARBOOK...
MIND IF I TAKE A LOOK AT THIS?
YEARBOOK

FEEL FREE. YOU MIGHT AS WELL KEEP IT.
THE SAD TRUTH IS, NO ONE ELSE WILL WANT IT.

DOC?
SORRY TO INTERRUPT, BUT THE COPS ARE ON THE PHONE. THEY NEED YOU DOWNTOWN.

AGAIN?

UH-HUH.
SEEMS THERE'S BEEN ANOTHER MURDER.

THREE YEARS AGO...

...AS IS DISABLING THEIR SECURITY SYSTEMS AND RECORDING DEVICES. NOW...
...WHAT DO I **NEED?**

CLOTHING...

...FOOD AND WATER...

...A MAP...
USA
The NorthWest

...AND A MEANS TO **INTERACT** WITH THEIR SOCIETY.

A THOUSAND OF THEIR "DOLLARS" SHOULD SUFFICE FOR NOW...
AND THIS MACHINE CAN EASILY BE PERSUADED THAT NOTHING HAS BEEN TAKEN.
CASH

I DO NOT ***LIKE*** STEALING, BUT I HAVE NO CHOICE IF I AM TO SURVIVE. PERHAPS I CAN FIND A WAY TO REPAY THE STORES, AT LEAST?
BUT NOW I MUST FIND A PLACE TO ***HIDE***...

...AND IT COULD BE A ***LONG*** WAIT.
WHAT AM I GOING TO ***DO*** ON EARTH?

SO HOW LONG HAVE YOU WORKED FOR THE DECEASED?

NEARLY FIVE YEARS.
SEEMS LONGER.

I'M SORRY FOR YOUR LOSS, MA'AM, BUT--
LOSS?

HE WAS A CANTANKEROUS OLD **GOAT**, AND I'M GLAD I DON'T HAVE TO PUT UP WITH HIM ANYMORE.
'CEPTING I'M OUT OF A **JOB** NOW.

QUITE.
MAYBE YOU CAN JUST TELL ME WHAT HAPPENED HERE, AS FAR AS YOU KNOW.

WELL, I WAS READING, AND I HEARD A NOISE FROM HIS ROOM...
I THOUGHT HE'D FALLEN OUT OF BED. SO I WENT IN TO CHECK, AND...

I MUST HAVE LEFT MY **KNITTING** IN THERE, AND...
...AND...

YES, I SAW.
I REALIZE THIS MUST BE VERY UPSETTING FOR YOU, BUT **ANYTHING** YOU CAN TELL US WOULD--

HE WAS JUST STANDING THERE, LOOKING DOWN ON...
...ON WHAT HE'D **DONE**.

YOU SAW HIM? THE KILLER?
CAN YOU DESCRIBE HIM?

HE WAS...
...HE WAS...

NAKED?
REALLY?
THAT'S WHAT SHE SAID. COULDN'T GIVE US MUCH OF A DESCRIPTION BEYOND THAT, THOUGH...
...GUESS SHE GOT DISTRACTED.
WE GOT A BARE FOOTPRINT IN SOME BLOOD OVER HERE. KIND OF BACKS UP HER STORY.
YOU GUYS GET A PHOTO OF THIS YET?
WE GOT PHOTOS, SAMPLES, YOU NAME IT.
AND WE'RE DONE HERE.
HE'S ALL YOURS NOW.
WHO WAS HE?
CARTER BLAINE. USED TO RUN THE BANK IN TOWN. BEEN RETIRED TWENTY YEARS OR MORE.
MEAN OLD COOT. HALF THE TOWN HATED HIM.

WELL, THE CAUSE OF DEATH IS OBVIOUS.
STABBED WITH A KNITTING NEEDLE, RIGHT THROUGH THE HEART...WITH ALMOST ***SURGICAL*** PRECISION.

IT'S AS IF THE KILLER USED WHATEVER CAME TO HAND FOR A WEAPON...
JUST LIKE WITH HODGES. SO...THIS **COULD** PUT THE ROBERTS BOY IN THE CLEAR.
YEAH, I THINK THE CHIEF ***REALIZES*** THAT.

WHERE ***IS*** MIKE, ANYWAY?

"OUTSIDE, KICKING THE CAR.
"GONNA GIVE HIM ANOTHER TEN MINUTES BEFORE I TRY TALKING TO HIM AGAIN."

I **DEMAND** THAT YOU RELEASE MY CLIENT ***IMMEDIATELY***.

AND WHY SHOULD I DO THAT, PRAY TELL?

WHY, IT'S ALL OVER TOWN YOU HAD **ANOTHER** MURDER LAST NIGHT...
...WHILE MR. ROBERTS WAS UNDER LOCK AND KEY RIGHT HERE. HE COULDN'T POSSIBLY BE THE KILLER.

AND WHO SAYS THE TWO CASES ARE RELATED?
BESIDES, EVEN IF I CAN'T PROVE HE MURDERED DOC HODGES, WE ***STILL*** HAVE THE LITTLE RAT ON BURGLARY AND ILLEGAL POSSESSION OF PRESCRIPTION DRUGS.

YOUR CLIENT ISN'T GOING ***ANYWHERE***, GERALDINE.

AND THE LAST LINE, PLEASE.
A...Q... L...T...
E
H N
D F N
P T X Z
U Z D T F
D F N R T H

OKAY, THAT'S IT.
IT IS?
I THOUGHT THERE WAS MORE TO IT THAN THAT.

NOT IN YOUR CASE.
THERE'S ABSOLUTELY NOTHING WRONG WITH YOUR EYESIGHT. YOU HAVE NEAR-PERFECT VISION.
BUT...

THAT BLURRINESS YOU MENTIONED? PROBABLY JUST TIREDNESS.
TRY GETTING MORE SLEEP, MAYBE USE AN EYEWASH SOLUTION OCCASIONALLY.

WELL, CHEER UP--YOU'VE JUST BEEN SAVED THE COST OF A PAIR OF GLASSES.
YEAH...
...I GUESS.

WELL, SO FAR IT'S ALL **GOOD**, MR. MAXWELL.
OF COURSE, WE'LL HAVE TO WAIT FOR THE RESULTS OF THE BLOOD TEST, BUT IT SEEMS TO ME THAT YOU'RE IN PRACTICALLY **PERFECT** HEALTH.
COURSE I AM--AND CALL ME **BEN**.

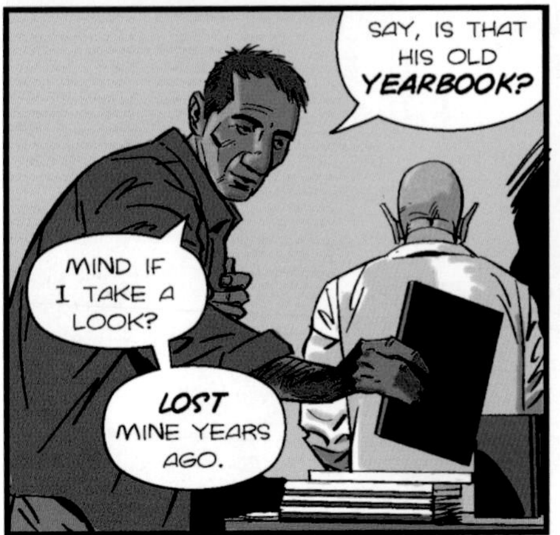

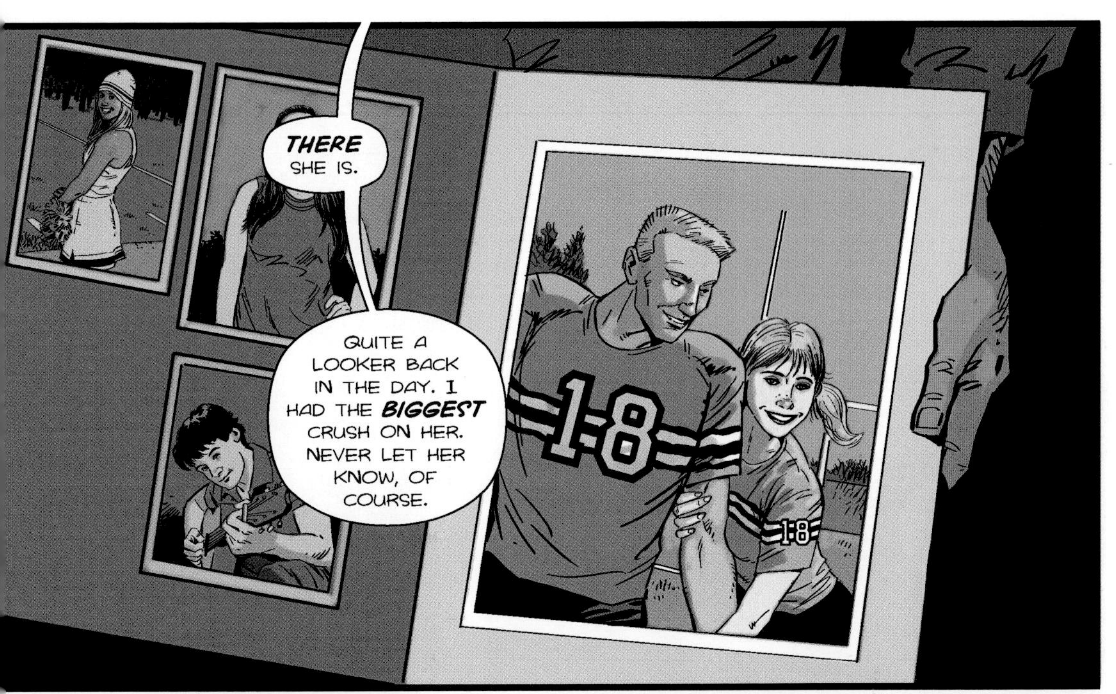
THERE SHE IS.
QUITE A LOOKER BACK IN THE DAY. I HAD THE BIGGEST CRUSH ON HER. NEVER LET HER KNOW, OF COURSE.
18
18

BUT... THAT ISN'T HODGES WITH HER...
NO -- THAT'S LANCE WHITEHEAD. SCHOOL'S STAR QUARTERBACK.
HE AND MARGIE WERE QUITE THE ITEM THAT YEAR.

BUT LANCE'S FOOTBALL SCHOLARSHIP FELL THROUGH, SO HE ENDED UP GETTING DRAFTED.
WE DID BASIC TRAINING TOGETHER. MY WAR WAS NOTHING SPECIAL, BUT HE CAME BACK FROM NAM A HERO. DECORATED, I MEAN.

BUT BY THEN MARGIE HAD TAKEN UP WITH SAM HODGES.
SURE SHE DIDN'T MEAN TO HURT LANCE...SHE JUST FELL IN LOVE. THESE THINGS HAPPEN, Y'KNOW?

I CAN'T ASK YOU TO WAIT.
I HAVE NO IDEA HOW LONG THIS TRIP WILL TAKE.
YOU DON'T HAVE TO ASK.
OF COURSE I'LL WAIT.
YES.
I SUPPOSE THEY DO.

SO... WHAT BECAME OF MR. WHITEHEAD?
POOR BASTARD.
THE BANK FORECLOSED ON HIS PARENTS' FARM WHILE HE WAS OVERSEAS...

...SO, WHAT WITH THAT AND MARGIE, THERE WAS NOTHING TO KEEP HIM HERE.

HEARD HE AND HIS FOLKS MOVED TO IDAHO, AND THAT LANCE MARRIED SOME GIRL HE MET OUT THERE.
BE NICE TO THINK SO.

WELL, THANKS FOR THE TRIP DOWN MEMORY LANE, DOC.
SEE YOU NEXT YEAR.

SO...
THERE'S NOTHING WRONG WITH MY EYES, SO...

Ophthalmic SURGERY

I'VE GOTTA TALK TO DAD.

EXCUSE ME?
WASN'T TALKING TO YOU.

IS IT **CURIOSITY** THAT IMPELS ME? **INTUITION?** OR JUST THE FACT THAT BECAUSE OF ALL THIS I AM NO LONGER **BORED?**
PERHAPS I'M TURNING **NATIVE?**

CAN I HELP YOU?
YES, I HOPE SO. I WAS WONDERING...DO YOU HAVE ANY OLD NEWSPAPERS HERE?
THE LOCAL ONE, I MEAN.

THE **POST?** SURE.
HOW OLD? WHAT YEAR ARE YOU LOOKING FOR?

THE EARLY 1970S.
OH, THAT'S ALL STILL ON MICROFICHE.

MACHINE'S THIS WAY.
I'LL SHOW YOU HOW IT WORKS.

AN ENGAGEMENT

Dr. and Mrs. Henry Wilkins are proud to announce the forthcoming wedding of their daughter Margaret to Samuel Hodges, son of Chester and Pamela Hodges on

...TO DISCOVER THAT HIS GIRLFRIEND NOW LOVES ANOTHER MAN...

FOR SALE BY AUCTION

LIVESTOCK, BUILDINGS, AND EQUIPMENT

The former Whitehead Farm, Frog Hollow Road - to take place on September 25th, 1972

...AND HIS CHILDHOOD HOME NOW BELONGS TO STRANGERS.

IF THESE MURDERS HAD HAPPENED FORTY YEARS AGO, WHITEHEAD WOULD MAKE A PERFECT SUSPECT, BUT **NOW?**
IT JUST DOESN'T MAKE SENSE.

COULD THIS ALL BE JUST **COINCIDENCE?**
BUT...IF IT ***IS*** HIM SOMEHOW, THEN WHY **NOW?**

AND DID ANYONE ***ELSE*** OFFEND HIM? IS HE GOING TO KILL **AGAIN?**
FIND WHAT YOU WERE LOOKING FOR?

I'M REALLY NOT SURE...
...BUT THANK YOU, ANYWAY.

DAD?
YOU GOT A MINUTE?

FOR MY GOTH PRINCESS? SURE.
WHAT'S UP?

WEIRD %$&*...
...AND SINCE YOU KNOW ABOUT WEIRD %$&*, YOU'RE ABOUT THE ONLY PERSON I CAN ASK.

LANGUAGE, GIRL.
WHAT KIND OF WEIRD... STUFF?

WELL, THERE'S THIS GUY, AND...

A BOY?
YOU'RE SEEING A BOY?

GEEZ, DAD, **NO**.
HE'S... JUST A GUY.

BUT HALF THE TIME WHEN I LOOK AT HIM, HIS FACE IS A **BLUR**.
I HAD AN EYE TEST, AND IT'S DEFINITELY NOT ME. IT'S **HIM**.

DAD, **NOBODY'S** FACE IS A &*%$ING BLUR.
NOBODY **HUMAN**, ANYWAY.

WHAT, THEN?
A SPIRIT?

HELL, **YOU'RE** THE MEDICINE MAN...
SHAMAN.
WHATEVER. ANYWAY, HE SEEMS LIKE FLESH AND BLOOD TO ME, SO...WHAT SHOULD I **DO** ABOUT ALL THIS?

WHY MUST YOU DO ANYTHING? DO YOU FEEL YOU ARE IN **DANGER?**
WELL, NO... BUT...

PERHAPS HE IS A VISITOR TO OUR WORLD. SUCH THINGS ARE NOT UNKNOWN.
WHAT DOES YOUR HEART TELL YOU ABOUT THIS PERSON?

KIND OF A HOKEY WAY TO PUT IT, BUT...
...IF IT WASN'T FOR THE BLUR THING, I'D SAY HE WAS A GOOD GUY. A GOOD DOCTOR.

HE'S THE NEW DOCTOR?
DOES ANYONE ELSE SEE WHAT YOU SEE?

I DON'T THINK SO. NOBODY'S SAID ANYTHING.
THEN PERHAPS YOU SEE IT BECAUSE THERE IS A BOND BETWEEN YOU.
AND WHAT'S THAT SUPPOSED TO MEAN?

HE'S A DOCTOR. YOU'RE A NURSE.
PERHAPS YOU ARE MEANT TO HELP HIM.

EVERYTHING OKAY?
SURE, IT'S AS QUIET AS THE GRAVE HERE.
ASTA'S ON TONIGHT. SHOULD BE HERE IN AN HOUR OR SO.

ELLEN, COULD YOU ASK YOUR MOTHER SOMETHING FOR ME?
SEE IF SHE REMEMBERS SOMEONE FROM HER SCHOOL DAYS NAMED **LANCE WHITEHEAD?**

THAT NAME RINGS A BELL.
THOUGHT SO. HE'S ONE OF **OURS**. HE AND HIS WIFE MOVED HERE FROM IDAHO ABOUT A YEAR AGO.

SAD STORY. SHE DIED A MONTH AFTER THEY GOT HERE. DOC PRESCRIBED **HIM** SOME SLEEPING PILLS AFTERWARDS, AND THAT'S THE LAST WE SAW OF HIM.

HE CAME BACK. IT **IS** HIM.
I'VE GOT TO GO **OUT** FOR A WHILE.
AGAIN?
I KNOW, BUT...HOLD THE FORT, WOULD YOU? I MAY BE SOME TIME.

Three years ago...
SIR!
OVER HERE.
I'M GOING TO NEED A CHOPPER WITH A WINCH-- ONE OF OURS-- AND A FLATBED TRUCK.
YOU FOUND IT?
YES, SIR.
WE SURE DID.

I SHOULD HAVE CALLED MIKE. SHARED MY SUSPICIONS WITH HIM.
BUT...

IT ALL SOUNDS SO FOOLISH.
I NEED TO SEE FOR MYSELF. TO BE *SURE*.

MR. WHITEHEAD? I WONDERED IF I MIGHT HAVE A WORD?
I'M YOUR NEW *DOCTOR*.

SURE, C'MON IN.
HOPE YOU DON'T MIND THE MESS...GUESS I'M **USED** TO IT.

GRAB YOURSELF A SEAT.
YOU WANNA DRINK?

THANK YOU, NO.
IT... DOESN'T AGREE WITH ME.

YOU POOR BASTARD.
GUESS **I'LL** HAVE TO DRINK FOR BOTH OF US.

SO... WHAT CAN I DO FOR YOU, DOC?

I WAS JUST A LITTLE... CONCERNED.
YOU NEVER RENEWED YOUR PRESCRIPTION FOR SLEEPING PILLS, SO I WANTED TO CHECK THAT YOU WERE OKAY...

THE PILLS, YEAH. I DIDN'T LIKE THE WAY THEY MADE ME FEEL ALL *FUZZY* IN THE MORNING.
FIGURE I'D STICK WITH MY NIGHTCAP, AND THE KIND OF HANGOVER I'M *USED* TO.

NO REFLECTION ON SAM HODGES, THOUGH.
GOOD MAN. GOOD DOCTOR. DIDN'T DESERVE TO DIE LIKE THAT.

YOU WENT TO SCHOOL WITH HIM, DIDN'T YOU?
YEAH. HE EVEN MARRIED AN OLD FLAME OF MINE.
ANCIENT FLAME, ACTUALLY. WE WERE JUST *KIDS* BACK THEN.

THINK SAM WAS KIND OF LOST WITHOUT HER.
KNOW THE FEELING.

YOUR WIFE PASSED... LAST YEAR?
LILY. YEAH.
WE'D JUST RETIRED HERE. HOPED WE HAD YEARS AND YEARS LEFT TOGETHER...DIDN'T WORK OUT THAT WAY.

TOO BAD SHE COULDN'T HAVE KIDS.
SHE'D HAVE BEEN GOOD AT IT.

THANKS FOR DROPPING BY, DOC, BUT I'M GONNA THROW YOU OUT NOW.
GETTIN' KINDA SLEEPY.
OF COURSE.

SEE? DON'T NEED THE PILLS. THE BOOZE WORKS JUST FINE.
WELL, JUST...TRY NOT TO OVERDO IT.

DOESN'T REALLY MATTER IF I DO, DOES IT?
GOOD NIGHT, DOC.

NOTHING.
ABSOLUTELY NOTHING.
HE WASN'T HIDING ANYTHING. HE WASN'T EVEN NERVOUS.
HE'S NOT THE KILLER.
HOW COULD I BE SO WRONG?
SOME DETECTIVE I AM--AND THE REAL KILLER'S STILL OUT THERE, SOMEWHERE.

HEY, AMANDA.
HI, BRAD...
GOT YOUR ORDER RIGHT HERE.
JOE'S DINER

BURGERS, FRIES, COKES.
YOU BOYS ARE EATING LATE TONIGHT.

WAY THE CHIEF'S RIDING US, WE'RE LUCKY TO EAT AT ALL.
CAN'T SEE IT LETTING UP TILL WE CATCH THIS GUY.

YOU WILL.
WHOLE TOWN'S BEHIND YOU.

JOE'S DINER
POL

HERE Y'GO.
SHE'S GOT A ***KID***, YOU KNOW.

WHAT?
JUST SAYIN', IS ALL.
WELL ***DON'T***. MIND YOUR OWN.

HEY, BOYS... YOU'RE ***UP***.
DRIVER REPORTED A MOTORCYCLIST ACTING WEIRD ON THE ROAD UP NEAR THE CLINIC.

SAID THE GUY GOT OFF HIS BIKE AND STARTED TAKING ALL HIS ***CLOTHES*** OFF...

DRIVE.

HI, DOC.
SORRY I'M SO LATE...
I WENT ON AN ERRAND.

A POINTLESS ERRAND, AS IT TURNED OUT.
THAT'S OKAY. IT'S QUIET AGAIN TONIGHT... BUT...

DOC... HARRY...
COULD I TALK TO YOU ABOUT SOMETHING? ONLY, THERE'S SOMETHING I NEED TO ASK YOU...

OF COURSE. JUST LET ME GET MYSELF A CUP OF--

WHAT WAS THAT?

WHAT?
I'M NOT SURE.

THOUGHT I HEARD A **NOISE** OUT THERE...
BE **CAREFUL**, DOC.

NO... IT'S OKAY.
I CAN'T SEE ANYTHIN--

ekk

COME...
...ON.

NOSY, NOSY.
CAN'T HAVE THAT.
errgh

LET HIM GO.
NOW.

YOU'RE NEXT, SQUAW.
CLIK
BLANG!

nyaaagh
GEEZ...
SORRY, DOC. THIS TIME.
CRAK

BLAMM!

PTOW!

POLICE!
GET **OFF** THE GIRL OR YOU'RE A DEAD MAN.

KEEP HER.
LOOKS LIKE I'M DONE HERE.

ASTA, GET ME A CLEAN TOWEL TO USE FOR A COMPRESS, THEN SEE TO MR. MAXWELL'S WOUND.

BUT...

I CAN WAIT. THE PATIENT COMES FIRST.

WOUND'S PRETTY CLEAN--BULLET WENT STRAIGHT THROUGH.
PRISON HOSPITAL CAN DEAL WITH THAT.
JUST PATCH HIM UP ENOUGH SO'S I CAN GET HIM THERE.

WHY'D YOU DO IT, BEN?
ALL THOSE PEOPLE...

DESERVED TO DIE.
AND I DID IT FOR LANCE, OF COURSE.

YOU'VE SEEN HIM. SEEN WHAT HE'S BECOME.
HE WAS A HERO, AND NOW HE'S... PATHETIC.

THOSE PEOPLE ROBBED HIM OF THE LIFE HE COULD HAVE HAD. THE LIFE HE DESERVED.
I JUST WANTED TO EVEN THE SCORE. GLAD I DID.

BEN, LANCE IS THE WAY HE IS BECAUSE...HIS WIFE JUST DIED, AND HE'S GRIEF STRICKEN AND LOST. HE DOESN'T CARE ABOUT THE PAST.
AND HE'D NEVER HAVE WANTED THIS.

OKAY, I GOTTA ASK...
WHY'D YOU DO IT NAKED?

WHEN YOU'RE NAKED, THE GOOKS CAN'T SEE YOU.

OH, GREAT-- AN INSANITY PLEA.
HE'S GOOD TO GO, CHIEF.

THEN LET'S GET THIS NUT OUT OF HERE, LEAVE YOU IN PEACE.
ASTA'LL FIX YOU UP, HARRY --RIGHT?
RIGHT.

OKAY, DOC...
LET'S GET YOU TO THE COUCH.

EASY DOES IT...
NO HURRY.
unnhh

SORRY. DIDN'T MEAN TO SHOOT YOU.
I... unh...KNOW THAT.
BULLET'S STILL IN THERE --IT'S GOT TO COME OUT.

I CAN DO IT. JUST...
...GIVE ME A MINUTE.

DON'T TALK CRAZY. YOUR HANDS ARE SHAKING, AND YOU'RE PROBABLY IN SHOCK.
I CAN DO IT. HELPED DOC HODGES ENOUGH TIMES.

NO, REALLY, ASTA, I CAN--
HARRY, SHUT UP.

LOOK, I UNDERSTAND.
YOU'RE WORRIED I MIGHT FREAK OUT IF I NOTICE SOMETHING... UNUSUAL.

BUT I ALREADY KNOW, OKAY?
I KNOW YOU'RE NOT... LIKE US.

what
did
you
say?

THREE YEARS AGO...

OKAY, LET'S GET A LOOK AT THIS THING.

YOU'RE MISSING ONE THING, SIR.
UP HERE.

THAT'S WHAT'S LEFT OF A SEAT.
THIS THING HAD A **PILOT**...

WE DIDN'T FIND ANY REMAINS. CHECKED THE WHOLE AREA...
...AND THERE WERE **FOOTPRINTS**, LEADING TO THE HIGHWAY.

THEN... I WANT HIM **FOUND**.
ALIVE, IF POSSIBLE.

SORRY, YOUR HONOR. ABSOLUTELY ***NOT***.
BUT I ONLY WANTED TO SEE HIM FOR A ***MINUTE***...

LOOK, THE POOR MAN HAD A BULLET TAKEN OUT OF HIM LAST NIGHT.
HE NEEDS ***REST***.

er, I BROUGHT SOME CANDY...
I'LL SEE THAT HE GETS IT... ***AND*** YOUR BEST WISHES.

WELL, IT'S GOOD TO SEE HIM SMILING, ANYWAY...
YEAH, MORPHINE WILL ***DO*** THAT.
NOW ***SCOOT***.

IT'S SO PEACEFUL HERE, JUST DRIFTING.
I FEEL HAPPY. I FEEL SAFE.
IS THIS HOME?
OR...MY OTHER HOME?
HOW STRANGE...
DO I REALLY THINK OF PATIENCE AS HOME NOW?
IT DOESN'T MATTER. IT'S BEAUTIFUL, WHEREVER IT IS...
AND EVERYTHING ELSE CAN WAIT.
TO BE CONTINUED IN RESIDENT ALIEN VOLUME 2: THE SUICIDE BLONDE!

WHO'S THAT MAN?

AFTERWORD BY PETER HOGAN
WITH ART BY STEVE PARKHOUSE

I blame Elvis Presley. Many years ago, I edited a book about the man, and got fascinated by Alfred Wertheimer's photographs from the early days of his career. These showed Presley in everyday settings like diners and hotels, traveling on trains and hanging around in stations—and the truly remarkable thing about them was the fact that all the other people in those photographs were completely ignoring Elvis, despite the fact that he looked nothing like anyone else in the room (or on the planet, for that matter). It was like there was a Martian in town, and they just couldn't see him.

Perhaps that's why one of the first images that occurred to me for *Resident Alien* was of Harry sitting in a diner, surrounded by other people—but being ignored by them. It's an idea Steve Parkhouse worked up in this early developmental sketch, and he returned to it later for the cover of issue #1. I think it's really powerful. In a way, it tells you the whole story concept right there.

So, the next time you're in a diner, take a good look around you. You might be surprised at who you see.

—PETER HOGAN
STILL STUCK ON EARTH, 2012

Resident Alien #0 front cover—April 2012.

Resident Alien #1 front cover—May 2012.

Resident Alien #2 front cover—June 2012.

Resident Alien #3 front cover—July 2012.